RECOLLECTIONS

OF

CHARLES KIRK,

Late of Warminster, Pennsylvania. An Elder in the
Society of Friends. Written in his
Seventy-ninth Year.

PRINTED FOR
THE JANE JOHNSON TRUST
BY
FRIENDS' BOOK ASSOCIATION,
FIFTEENTH AND RACE STREETS, PHILADELPHIA.
1892.

HARVARD COLLEGE LIBRARY
GIFT OF
FRIENDS HISTORICAL LIBRARY
SWARTHMORE COLLEGE
JAN 16 1935

PREFACE.

WE believe there are few who were acquainted with the subject of the following recollections that will not be interested in perusing the incidents of his practical and dedicated life, and we trust their simple narration may be an encouragement to others to persevere in the path of right and duty, and strengthen them to hold fast their confidence in the Divine Arm of Power that will assuredly sustain them under all circumstances.

H. E. K.

Philadelphia, Twelfth month, 1891.

CONTENTS.

CHAPTER I.

Some account of his ancestors—His Birth—Yellow Fever in Philadelphia—Crippled condition of his father—Telling his father a falsehood—Enlarging the home—Cold summer of 1816—Death of his mother—Sickness in the family—Effects of the introduction of paper money—His ardent temperament. 1

CHAPTER II.

Customs in farmers' families in the early part of the century—His first carriage—Trip to Niagara Falls—Marriage of his sister Ruth—Marriage of his sister Phebe—Accident to his brother Aaron—Separation in the Society of Friends—His marriage to Elizabeth Conard—Their first home—His sickness, ... 14

CHAPTER III.

Death of his sister and father—Breaking up of his childhood's home—Marriages of two of his brothers—His conclusion to attend mid-week meetings—Sacrifices in abstaining from slave produce—Practical sympathy extended to a friend—A slave girl received into his home—Marriage of his brother Abraham—Marriage of his sister Rachel—Removal to Shoemakertown—Settlement in Warminster Township, Pa.—Long attendance at the Philadelphia Market—Death of his wife's father—Religious visit with Elizabeth Newport to the families of Wrightstown Monthly Meeting, etc., ... 22

CHAPTER IV.

Religious visit with Ann Weaver—Constitution of Texas that Slavery shall never be abolished—Death of a near neighbor—Religious visit with E. Newport in 1845—Helping a neighbor to provide a home for his family—Death of his wife's mother—Visit with E. Newport 1850—Building a house for the widow and fatherless—Visit with E. Newport 1852—Visit with E. Newport 1853 and 1854—Death of his sister Ruth—Marriage of his son—Visit with E. Newport in 1857—Drouth in the summer of 1858—Visit with E. Newport in 1861—Visit to Loudoun county, Virginia, 1867, ... 33

CHAPTER V.

Religious visit to Ohio Yearly Meeting—Death of his wife—Family visits with M. E. Travilla to the members of Abington Monthly Meeting—Visits to the families of Westbury Monthly Meeting, L. I., as companion for M. E. T. and Martha Dodgson—His regular attendance at his own meeting—His interest in organizations of practical value in his neighborhood—His marriage to Harriet E. Stockly, of Philadelphia—Visits to meetings under an

CONTENTS.

appointment of the Yearly Meeting's Committee on Education—Attends Ohio Yearly Meeting—Attends some meetings in the Western States—Attends Baltimore Yearly Meeting—His sickness there—His interest in the Public Library of Hatboro—Attends Genesee Yearly Meeting—Attends New York Yearly Meeting—Attends Baltimore Yearly Meeting, ... 44

CHAPTER VI.

His strong testimony against the use of intoxicants—Attends Centre Quarterly Meeting—Death of a sister-in-law—Attends meetings under an appointment of the Yearly Meeting's Committee on Deficiencies—Death of Susan M. Parrish—Religious visit to Friends of Purchase Quarterly Meeting, N. Y.—Visits by appointment of his Yearly Meeting to many of its meetings—Attends Baltimore Yearly Meeting—Attends New York Yearly Meeting—Death of Dillwyn Parrish—His sudden illness—Attends his Yearly Meeting for the last time—Attends Salem Quarterly Meeting, N. J.—His last sickness—His release from earth, ... 54

RECOLLECTIONS

OF

CHARLES KIRK.

CHAPTER I.

Some account of his ancestors—His Birth—Yellow Fever in Philadelphia—Crippled condition of his father—Telling his father a falsehood—Enlarging the home—Cold summer of 1816—Death of his mother—Sickness in the family—Effects of the introduction of paper money—His ardent temperament.

AMONG the papers of the late Charles Kirk, of Warminster, Bucks county, Pa., are the following memoranda, written from memory in his 79th year:

My ancestor, on my father's side, was John Kirk, who came from Derbyshire, England; was married to Joan Elliott, and bought five hundred acres of land in Upper Darby, on which they settled in 1687, and on which he lived until his death. He left the farm on which he resided to his son

William, and divided his property, in Montgomery county, among his other children.

His second son, John, my great-great-grandfather, located in Abington township, where he finally came into possession of seven hundred and fifty acres of land, on which, in 1735,[1] he built a large stone house, which is at this time in good condition. He married Sarah, daughter of Reynear Tyson, one of the German Friends that came from Cresheim, and settled at Germantown in 1683.

My grandfather, Jacob Kirk, had the homestead, on which he lived to the age of 93, and died in the house in which he was born; his twin brother, Isaac, lived on the adjoining tract, and died in his 91st year. I remember that my grandfather was a kind-hearted, industrious, and generous man, and very interesting in conversation. His deportment toward us children was gentle and courteous; he made us feel so happy that it is sweet to recall the time spent in his society. I recollect hearing him relate that his grandfather, Reynear Tyson, was not married when he first came to this country, and being disposed to marry his first

---

[1] This house is in Abington township, (Montgomery county, Pa.), near the line of Upper Dublin township, on a farm now belonging to Daniel Williams, and occupied by his son Alfred. The dwelling as it now stands was in part erected by John Kirk, in 1735; it was remodeled by his grandson, John Kirk, in 1822.

CHARLES KIRK.

cousin, and our Discipline not allowing it, they made preparation to go back to Germany to accomplish their marriage, but Friends seeing their sincerity, allowed them to proceed. I believe it may have been so, for I find by William Penn's "Travels in Germany," in 1667, that there were established meetings, and their rules of government may have been different from ours. We know that these German Friends were faithful to their convictions, for they were the first to bear a testimony against slavery.

My mother, Rebecca Iredell, was the great-granddaughter of Thomas Iredell, who came recommended by certificate from the Monthly Meeting at Pardshaw Crag, Cumberland, England, "ye 27th of 6th mo. 1700."

John Cadwallader, who came from Wales, and was a minister of some note in the Society of Friends, was also a great-grandfather of my mother. He traveled considerably in the service of Truth, and about the year 1742 went to the West Indies on a religious visit, and died there about the same time that Thomas Chalkley and John Estaugh ended their days there, and was buried in the same grave, on the island of Tortola. When George Truman, John Jackson, and Thomas B. Longstreth visited the island on a similar mission they saw the graves.

My parents, Jacob and Rebecca Kirk, lived in Abington township, Montgomery county, Pa., one mile west of Willow Grove, and had eleven children. I was the fifth child and oldest son, and was born 10th of Twelfth month, 1800.

The summer after the marriage of my parents the yellow fever prevailed in Philadelphia to an alarming extent. Many died from its effects, and all that could do so left the city. It was a sorrowful time. I heard my mother say that for eight or nine weeks the latter part of the summer they had no rain except a slight sprinkle occasionally; the grass became dead and dry, and it was difficult to walk on it if the ground was ascending.

My father was a large, athletic man, capable of performing a great amount of physical labor, which he continued to do until about the year 1800, when, from various accidents, he became so crippled that he could not walk without a cane, and many things he could not do. While he was able he made great improvements on the farm; built a good, substantial cellar barn, the first in the neighborhood, and did various things in the way of improving the place, but when he was unable to work, things took a backward turn, and continued to go in that direction for several years.

I do not suppose the experiences of my life were very different from others, but my trials, conflicts, and I may say pleasures, have left their impress on my mind. The first of importance that I recall was telling my father a falsehood, and from that time to the present I have never been able to recur to it without horror and regret. In a few years after, when I read in the Bible the account of Jacob deceiving his old, blind father, it struck my mind with surprise and horror, and I have never read it from that day to this but a degree of the same feeling pervades my mind, and it appears that Jacob, too, suffered for his transgression and had to flee for his life, and even after twenty years had passed he was afraid to meet his brother Esau. My experience with regard to this untruth is, that its effects on my mind may be compared to a burn; it may get well, but the scar will remain. We may again come near to our Heavenly Father, and walk in his paths, but the recollection of our disobedience will remain with us. I can refer to no time in my life, even in childhood, when the Good Spirit was not present with me, reproving me when I did wrong, and speaking peace to my soul when I did right.

Being the oldest son I was put to do many things before I was fully able. In saying this I do not mean to reflect on my parents, but the necessity of the case seemed to require it, for, though the farm contained nearly one hundred acres, there was scarcely enough raised on it to meet the expenses of our large family. Many farmers, at that time, did not consider it necessary to enrich their land in order to make it produce. I remember my grandfather pointing to one of the fields and saying that nothing had been put on it for forty years. In the early part of the nineteenth century there was a large portion of land that had been productive when first cleared, but by continued cropping had become so exhausted the crops would not pay for gathering. The more enterprising farmers were beginning to put lime on the land, which made a wonderful change in the crops. I recollect mowing on our farm a good swath of clover where there had been nothing but lime put on, and where previous to that no crop of any kind would grow.

Early in my teens I accompanied my mother to market, but as I was too small to back up the wagon I had to ask some one to do it for me, which tried me exceedingly to have to be so beholden to others, but it taught me a lesson I have never forgotten, and that is to "feel another's woe."

For some time the house had been too small for the family, so in 1815 it was concluded to build an addition. This made a hard summer for us, for I had the stone to haul, besides other work. One day, the stone tender being absent, I had to take his place. It took all the strength I had, and I still remember that day's work. Fifty-five years after I again tended one of the same masons on my own farm.

On New Year's day, 1816, there being good sleighing, I was sent to Germantown with a sled-load of wood for sale, which felt to me to be a great undertaking. There were between thirty and forty acres of heavy timber on our farm, and that was one resource in time of need, and as coal had not then been discovered and applied to domestic use, wood was in good demand for fuel.

The summer of this year, 1816, was the coldest ever known in this country. We had frost in every month. I remember seeing in the Sixth month the leaves on the hickory trees dead and crisp from the effects of it. The crops were very light; scarcely any corn came to maturity. These things touched me to the very quick, for I was so ashamed to be seen hauling hay in the spring of the year to feed our stock that I disliked to meet any one, for it seemed to my mind to manifest a want of industry and management. But I have lived to see that this kind of schooling, hard as it was to bear, had its good effect upon my mind.

I now come to the most sorrowful period of my life. In the latter part of the summer of this year my dear mother was taken sick with what was then called typhus fever, and after nine days of suffering, her trials and anxieties came to a close, and I fully believe she entered into a state of happiness. Here I must pause, for I have no words to convey the feelings of my mind on that occasion, and now, though more than sixty-two years have passed, the remembrance of it is so clear and strong, that I can scarcely refrain from shedding tears while writing these lines. At the time of her death there were ten children living, the youngest about four years of age. As we were not permitted to go into her room, I used to go and peep at her through a crack in the partition, and the impression on my mind was that if she were taken from us there would be no pleasure for me in this world; but I had not then learned to look to a higher Power for peace and happiness,—the great fountain and source of all good,—the sure foundation to build upon in this life. The children all took the fever; eight of them were sick in bed at one time; one of them, a girl of twelve years old, died; some of our neighbors were afraid to come near us, but others rendered us every assistance in their power. As I was the only one able to go, much fell to my lot to do. The doctors, at that time, depended almost wholly on stimulants; wine and brandy were used in large quantities, and I also had to go and solicit persons to sit up with the sick. This was a lesson of instruction to me which I have endeavored to profit by, that is, if any of the neighbors are sick, not to wait to be sent for, but to go and see if I can render any service. Grandmother Iredell lived in the family, and was of great use, for her meek and quiet spirit enabled her to have great control over us. She died in 1823.

The religious feeling of my mother was strong and deep. From my early childhood she was careful to attend all our religious meetings; as we had but one carriage, which held only three persons, she was anxious to have a larger conveyance, so that more of her children could attend meeting with her. After a few years we got a two-horse carriage, and although we lived four miles from meeting, a full load went regularly twice a week. The recollection of going and sitting by her side in meeting is still fresh in my mind.

After I was nine years old I never went to school except for about three months in the winter season; the rest of the year I was kept at work, but by close attention I made considerable progress in study, so that I went through the arithmetic, mensuration, surveying, and algebra, and of all these I had a good knowledge, except the last.

After the general sickness and the two deaths in our family, we had a hard struggle. The doctor's bills were upwards of $180, besides a large store bill for wine, brandy, and other things, and our resources were quite small, but we had been accustomed to work, and we applied ourselves faithfully to it, and by strict economy, in not very many months the bills were all paid, and in doing this we all learned a lesson, which has been useful to us through life. I have often thought if we had called a half-dozen men together and presented to them our liabilities and resources, they would have said, " you cannot accomplish this thing ; " but we did, for we worked hard, and lived economically.

In 1816 my father bought fourteen acres of land adjoining his farm, on which we raised wheat which we sold at $2.50 a bushel. The war with England (of 1812 and 1814) and Bonaparte's ravages in Europe, made paper money plenty, and things became inflated. Wheat sold at $3.00 a bushel ; and other produce in proportion, but when the reaction came, after 1816, wheat sold at 72 cents per bushel, corn and rye at 28 cents, oats 16 and 20 cents per bushel, and other things at similar prices, which made hard times for farmers. Many who had saved money during the time of high prices, had bought farms, and paid one-half the purchase money, had finally to be sold out by the sheriff, and it was several years before stability and confidence were restored.

The next fall we commenced to haul wood to the kiln. It took fifteen cords of wood to burn one thousand bushels of lime, and the person who furnished wood enough to burn the kiln had one-half of the lime. I have always thought the lime-burner had the best of the bargain. At that time lime sold at the kiln for 25 and 30 cents a bushel. A year or two later we opened an abandoned limestone quarry on the southern part of our farm, and by hiring a man who understood blasting rocks, we got stone enough to burn a kiln of lime, and I learned that kind of work, and had plenty of lime for a while.

Our farm was a stony one, and the picking of stone to prepare the ground for mowing was a tedious job. There was so much sameness in it, and the days seemed so long, it was a thing I used to dread, but let no one accept from my reference to these occurrences that my life was a hard one. I do not remember a time when I did not take pleasure in doing things for the benefit of myself and others. I feel that it has been a blessing to me to have had a little mirth and humor incorporated into my composition, though this cast of mind was one that required me to keep on the watch, for I was often inclined to be sarcastic; that, together with my quick, ardent, hasty temperament, has kept me sinning and repenting all my life; but then, my sense of the rights of others and my conscientiousness, have always brought repentance, for I never gave an unkind word or did an unkind act but I felt regret for it, and often have I endeavored to seek reconcilation with Heaven's recording spirit, and would have to go to the person to whom I gave offense before peace would be fully restored.

CHAPTER II.

Customs in farmers' families in the early part of the century—His first carriage—Trip to Niagara Falls—Marriage of his sister Ruth—Marriage of his sister Phebe—Accident to his brother Aaron—Separation in the Society of Friends—His marriage to Elizabeth Conard—Their first home—His sickness.

IN 1820 times had not changed much. This summer I brought butter home from the Philadelphia market because we could not get ten cents a pound for it; and this was the experience of others besides myself. Being offered twenty cents a bushel for oats this summer, and as that was one and a quarter cents above the average, we went to work and threshed it with a flail,—for there were no threshing machines in those days. At that time farmers' implements were very inferior to what they now are, and the boys were generally given the poorest ones. My first experience in loading hay was when I was ten years old, and as I had no fork or any other implement, I reached out my arms to receive it. It was the custom in those days for farmers' families to dress in home-spun, which was flax woven into linen, and wool into "linsey."

Each year it took about one acre of flax to furnish the family with clothing; this involved a great amount of labor. When the ground was dry, pulling the flax was a hard, back-aching job; then beating the seed off was tedious and troublesome. The whole process of its preparation was slow and rough, but there seemed no help for it, as what was then called "domestic goods" had not come into general use. Some calico was imported from the East Indies; I remember my sisters paying seventy-five cents a yard for it. At that time six yards made a dress. Cotton was not of much value until after the invention of Whitney's cotton gin in 1793, and it was years before machinery for carding and spinning was brought to perfection, so as to supersede the use of flax.

1821. A very mild winter; ground not much frozen, but plenty of mud. The farm by this time was very much improved. Our horses not being suitable for a young man to drive, my father gave me a fine, three-year-old colt, and said I might cut and haul wood enough to pay for a saddle and bridle, which I very much appreciated. I never went into young company until after I was twenty-one. The reason was because there were so very few I desired to make much acquaintance with, on account of their mode of living. At the time I am referring to, there were four young men in the neighborhood just about my age, who spent a good deal of their time and money at the tavern, which I was not disposed to do. These four all became bankrupt in purse and reputation, and died many years ago; and I can count scores of this class, whilst those who kept clear of these things and pursued lives of honest industry and economy have all acquired homes of their own and have been comfortable through life.

The summer of 1822 was very dry, and vegetation very much dried up for want of rain. As I had not a carriage of my own, my father proposed that I should quarry out stone, burn a kiln, and sell enough lime to buy one. It took about twenty cords of wood to burn a kiln, but it was all accomplished without extra hiring, and after fifty years' observation I am fully persuaded that if more young men had to pass through a similar experience it would be better for them. In the fall of this year my friend Daniel Longstreth and I planned a trip to Niagara Falls. We each furnished a horse to our new, light wagon, and, with my sister Phebe and our friend Sarah Ann Ely, we left home on a Second-day morning, in the early part of the Tenth month, and reached Easton that night, and on the following Seventh-day afternoon we arrived at S. A. Ely's uncle's, Thomas Hutchinson's, a distance of 220 miles from our homes, and received a warm welcome. The expense of traveling in that new country was very small. Our provisions we carried with us, as was the custom at that time, and on arriving at the tavern took our seats at the long table, opened our knapsacks, called for tea or coffee, for which the charge was six cents apiece, and paid six cents each for a night's lodging.

On First-day we attended Scipio Meeting, and on Second-day morning Daniel and I started for the Falls, going through Rochester, then a comparatively new place, where we remained over night, made some stop at Lockport, and on Seventh-day afternoon arrived at Niagara Falls. This cannot be described, but must be seen to be realized. The rapids are almost as wonderful as the Falls. On our return we again visited Thomas Hutchinson's, where we had left the girls, spent a few days in looking around the country, and reached our homes in good health, after an absence of four weeks, at an expense of $28 for my sister and myself.

The year 1823 was a more plentiful season than we had had for several years: rains copious and in due season. In the Eleventh month of this year sister Ruth was married to Charles Thomas, of Hatboro. The giving her a reasonable "outfit" involved some expense, but we were enabled to do it to good satisfaction. My only object in referring to these things is to show how much can be accomplished by industry and economy. Our pecuniary affairs were now much brighter; the farm was very much improved; the family more comfortable, and I felt at liberty to enjoy the society of my young friends, of whom I was very fond, especially of some of my female friends. In the summer of 1824 my oldest sister, Phebe, married Joseph Paxson, who lived near Wilmington, Delaware. The marriage was accomplished at Upper Dublin meeting-house the day after monthly meeting, Friends appointing a special meeting for the purpose. When the time came for our sister to say farewell every one in the house was in tears, and I soon found I could not bear up under the general feeling, so I got into the wagon and drove off with my load, and had a crying spell all to myself. I suppose we felt the parting from her more deeply as she had been the housekeeper since our dear mother's death, and although it had been eight years since that event, the wound was not healed, but ready to bleed at every occurrence that called it to mind. The marriages of my two sisters occurring so near together put us under the necessity of borrowing to accomplish the outfit of the last one, but the next year the money was all paid back.

The year 1825 passed without any occurrence of special interest, but the summer of 1826 was a very dry one. We had no rain till about the 20th of the Sixth month; except the first year's mowing and the meadow land, the grass did not make more than a half ton per acre. The oats were scarcely worth gathering. Great was the delight when the clouds in the south and southwest began to thicken and the wind changed to the east by way of the south, a sure indication of rain. The wind often goes to the east by way of the north, but it will never bring rain in dry weather. This summer our brother Aaron met with a serious accident. While engaged in working with a circular saw, in attempting to remove a chip out of the way, his thumb was caught, his hand badly lacerated, and his shoulder put out of joint. For three months his sufferings were very great, and every week I went once or oftener, several miles, to sit up with him. He finally recovered, and, although disabled, became a successful farmer. Though he had been for sometime in business for himself, those of us at home felt it right to pay his bills for medical attendance.

Our next neighbor having more land than he farmed, I planted, with his consent, some eight or ten acres with corn, for which I had half the crop. This was done without neglecting anything at home, and I realized about $85 by the operation, and half of the fodder besides. The year 1827 was marked by an unhappy controversy in the Society of Friends in regard to doctrinals. What one portion considered sound and edifying, the other portion pronounced unsound and spurious, and this finally caused a separation. In Horsham Monthly Meeting the relative proportion of the two branches was one " Orthodox " to seventeen of our Friends; in our yearly meeting nine thousand of the former (O.) and there were more than eighteen thousand of our Friends.

As the family at home was so situated that I could be spared, I began to look toward forming a marriage connection. The marriage took place with Elizabeth, daughter of Jonathan and Hannah Conard, on the 13th of Twelfth month of this year, in Horsham meeting-house, in the presence of a large company of friends and relatives, and on the 5th of Third month, 1828, we settled on a rented farm which George Peterson of Philadelphia had then recently bought, located on the county line, seven miles from the city, containing sixty-four acres, about four of which were woodland. The property had previously belonged to three single sisters, who had let it become so reduced that the year before we moved on it there had not been a plow put in it because it was too poor to pay for farming.

Our landlord had the capital and we the capacity to labor, and we went on harmoniously, which is the true principle of business. Our start in life was a very moderate one. I think the money value of all we both had would not have exceeded eight hundred dollars, but we were content to begin with little rather than go in debt. By pursuing this course we were enabled by degrees to add various things to our scanty outfit, and at the end of the year had two hundred dollars to place out on interest. It was during the first years of my married life that I made, what felt to me like a covenant with my Heavenly Father, that if I ever acquired a home worth ten thousand dollars I would be fully satisfied, and would not covet any more.

In the Third month of the following year, 1829, I had a severe spell of bilious pleurisy, and my cough continued for some weeks. This was a discouraging time, for I felt that our means of living depended on my labor, and the prospect of being disabled and dependent on others was sad; but after a time my health was restored, and I truly returned thanks to my Heavenly Father for this great blessing.

CHAPTER III.

Death of his sister and father—Breaking up of his childhood's home—Marriages of two of his brothers—His conclusion to attend mid-week meetings—Sacrifices in abstaining from slave produce—Practical sympathy extended to a friend—A slave girl received into his home—Marriage of his brother Abraham—Marriage of his sister Rachel—Removal to Shoemakertown—Settlement in Warminster Township, Pa.—Long attendance at the Philadelphia Market—Death of his wife's father—Religious visit with Elizabeth Newport to the families of Wrightstown Monthly Meeting, etc.

As I am writing altogether from memory, I have failed to record exactly in the order of time the death of my beloved sister Hannah, in the early part of this year. She was lovely, gentle, and kind, and it was a sore bereavement. A dear cousin, who had been in poor health for some time, and grandfather Kirk both died in the Tenth month of this year, and were buried on the same day, one aged 29, the other 93 years.

1830. My health having been restored far beyond my expectations, or that of any of my friends, we applied ourselves closely to business. I farmed the sixty-four acres with only two horses, and for two years I hauled eighty loads of manure each year from the city, and one year one hundred loads of all kinds,—lumber and other things included. I did not keep a hired man,—only a boy. We took one when he was about ten years old, and kept him till he was sixteen, for his board and clothing and three months' schooling in the winter. For several years, through mowing and harvest, I exchanged work with the neighbors and thus got along without hiring.

1831. The farm much improved and things quite comfortable. When we first went there we felt so poor and the land was so poor, we thought the neighbors, who were all rich and had good farms and investments besides, would not take much notice of us, but they all came to visit us, and continued to do so as long as their health permitted, and I am inclined to believe if we act well our part we will always be respected.

In the summer of this year our father, who had gradually become more crippled, was suddenly smitten with apoplexy, which terminated his life in about twenty-four hours. This caused the breaking up of the family. He left a will dividing his estate equally amongst us, except that he bequeathed me four hundred dollars for my services to the family, which I thought too much, and, as sister Phebe had kept house eight years, I offered her fifty dollars of it, which she declined. I also offered the brother that hurt his hand fifty dollars, which he accepted. This was the way we acted towards each other, and the estate was settled without the aid of a lawyer.

After our father's death we all thought it best to sell the farm and the personal property, which was done that fall. The night after the sale we four brothers made beds on the floor and remained in the house, but the emotions and reflections of my mind were such that "sleep came not to my eyes, nor slumber to my eyelids," for the night was spent in a review of all the scenes of my life up to that time. This selling out and breaking up of the home was capping the climax. A sad and mournful night it was to me; no one in my life had been more so. The same fall my brother Samuel was married to Martha Paul, and settled in Byberry. In the spring of 1832 our son was born, and named for my cousin, Wm. J. Kirk. This event, I felt, greatly increased our responsibilities. In the autumn of this year brother Aaron was married to Ann Paul, sister of Martha, and the next year he bought a part of the Governor Keith tract in Horsham, and moved into the old mansion house, of which our great-grandfather did the mason work one hundred and ten years previously.

1833. Since we commenced housekeeping we had been diligent in the attendance of our religious meetings on First-days and monthly meetings, but not of those held on week-days, but now we felt the time had come for us to attend these also. It required considerable struggle to leave the work, especially in the busy season, but I can truly say, after more than fifty years' experience, I have never lost anything, but have succeeded in temporals as well as those who staid at home, and I am fully convinced that every right endeavor will be blessed, and O, how I desire to impress upon all members the duty of attending all our religious meetings! No society or association can exist long if its meetings are not kept up. These opportunities are often seasons of instruction to the mind. At a week-day meeting when no outward voice was heard, I was convinced that it was not right for me to partake of the produce of slave labor, to which conviction I endeavored to be faithful. The difficulty and expense of obtaining free produce was considerable, but that was very small compared with the feeling it occasioned in other minds on account of our not partaking of what they sat before us. I often thought if they would only pass us by without comment how much more satisfactory it would be. Not many seemed to appreciate or understand the motive, and not unfrequently I received a retort calculated to grate on the feelings. In our Religious Society the pro-slavery feeling abounded to a great extent. We can sometimes best exemplify the condition of things by stating facts. On one occasion we were visiting a mutual friend, and our pleasure was almost spoiled because we did not partake of articles of food which were the products of slave labor. The wife, in tone and manner not very kindly, remarked: " You do not eat of anything we have," because we did not partake of all that was set before us, and during the afternoon the husband said that " no one who was an abolitionist could have any appointment in their monthly meeting," and this was the feeling of many who professed to be Friends. Few who did not live at that time could imagine the state of things. There were two extremes: and Truth suffered between them.

In 1834, about the middle of the Fifth month, we had an extremely cold spell of weather for the season. All the corn that was above ground was killed, and the clover frozen, but they were not seriously hurt,—only retarded for a time. The next two years I do not call to mind much that will interest others, except that in 1836 the wheat crop was very poor. The yield was not sufficient to bread the inhabitants, and a large quantity was imported from Europe, and this large importation from other countries, together with bad management in public affairs, brought on a suspension of specie payments in the following year, and a general loss of confidence.

In 1838, a friend of mine who had previously been a wild, profane man, but who had become convinced of Friends' principles and testimonies, and had come forth in the ministry, finding that business in the city with the small means at his command was rendered more difficult by his convictions in regard to many things in connection therewith, which he thought were not conducive to his growth in better things, had concluded to move into the country. He bought a farm in New Jersey, which put him considerably in debt, and feeling unity and sympathy with him, I offered to lend him some money, which he gladly accepted, and often, in later years, he referred to it with gratitude. How much more good might be done than there is, if we were so disposed! The latter part of this summer was very dry,—not enough rain to wet the ground plough-deep till the middle of the Ninth month. In the fall of this year our daughter was born, and named for her maternal grandmother.

About two years previous to the time last referred to, one evening just before dark, Mary and Susan Cox, who then lived at Germantown, came to our house with a colored girl about twelve years old, fresh from slavery, whom they called Susan Lewis, for us to take care of and keep her from the kidnappers. By the aid of some one who understood the business, she and her family, consisting of seven or eight persons, had been brought from Page county, beyond Winchester, Va., and located in Philadelphia. The kidnappers searched them out, and one evening seized them and took them all back into slavery, except this Susan, who just at that time had been sent on an errand. That night she was taken in haste to Germantown, and the next night brought to our house. We did not need her, but we kept her, and she lived with us till she was eighteen, and several years after. She was a good, faithful, honest girl, and while in our employ saved several hundred dollars, upon which I paid her interest. With the view of making more money she went to Philadelphia, and finally married respectably.

In the early part of the year 1839 our brother Abraham was married to Caroline Jarrett, and not long after our Sister Rachel entered into the marriage relation with Richard Knight, of Byberry. Her previous home having been broken up by the marriage of her brother, we invited them to have their wedding entertainment at our house, which they accepted. At that time it was the custom to have wine on such occasions, but as we felt an objection to its use and they were willing to dispense with it, it was omitted, and we all realized peace and satisfaction therefrom. This was the first wedding without wine of which I had any knowledge.

We had now lived on a rented farm twelve years, and by industry and economy had accumulated six thousand dollars, averaging five hundred dollars a year, and we felt disposed to invest our earnings in a farm, but on looking around with that object we found none that suited us; so for one year we rented a small farm at Shoemakertown and moved on it the first of Fourth month, 1840, thinking as it was a small place we would have time to visit our neighbors and friends. But in this we were disappointed, for we never could leave home but that the boys from the village would assemble at our place, or our boy would take the opportunity to go away.

In the summer of 1840 Friends' meeting-house at Warminster, Pa., was built, and in the succeeding fall I bought a farm of nearly 119 acres within one mile of it, for $10,529.89. The farm was a desirable one, with good buildings, a fair proportion of timber, and in a good neighborhood, but it was a sore trial to separate from our friends at Abington, to whom we had become very much attached. It seemed the place of our espousals, for though all my life a member of our Society, and attached to it from childhood, there was in that meeting something like Bethel, where God first met me; perhaps I had better say, where I adopted the principles and testimonies professed by our Society as my own, and which I have endeavored to carry out in my daily walk among men, though feebly, it must be confessed, for as I approach the end of my journey it does not seem as if I had done much good.

We moved to our new home in the spring of 1841, and I would gladly have taken five hundred dollars less than I gave for the property if I could have disposed of it. Separating from old friends and making new ones rested heavily on my mind, and, in addition to this, money matters were in a bad plight. President Andrew Jackson had refused to sign the re-charter of the United States Bank, and the State of Pennsylvania, or rather the Legislature, had re-chartered it with a capital of $32,000,000, which was more than any local bank could manage, and the consequence was it became insolvent. After the bank closed there was a very large amount of that paper in circulation, and it was almost the only kind, and finally it went down to twenty-eight cents on the dollar, which caused a great prostration in business. The other banks at one time issued, instead of bank-notes, a sort of certificate, which did not even promise to pay. In making my first payment on the farm I received and paid $2,400 of this paper,—as for calling it "money," that was not correct. For many months I carried a heavy heart, but as time rolled on I became reconciled to my situation, and finally attached to our home friends and neighbors, and now, to me, it is the most pleasant place I find.

I attended market in Philadelphia every week for fifteen years, driving to the city, a distance of eighteen miles, until 1856, when our son was married and took the farm.. During a great part of this time produce was very low, butter 12½ cents a pound, oats 25 to 33 cents, corn 45 to 50 cents, wheat 85 cents to $1 per bushel, hay as low as 37½ cents a hundred. (I have mentioned the lowest prices of all these articles.)

In the fall of this year my wife's father passed to the life beyond the grave, leaving the income of all he possessed to his wife, after her death to be equally divided among his nine children. As I was one of the executors, my duties were considerably increased by this appointment.

The next three years, though not by any means a blank, were not marked by any event of general interest, except that in the Twelfth month, 1843, I accompanied Elizabeth Newport and Mary H. Schofield (Child) on a religious visit to the families of Wrightstown Monthly Meeting, Pa., and of Kingwood, N. J., of which an account will be found in the " Memoirs of Elizabeth Newport."

CHAPTER IV.

Religious visit with Ann Weaver—Constitution of Texas that Slavery shall never be abolished—Death of a near neighbor—Religious visit with E. Newport in 1845—Helping a neighbor to provide a home for his family—Death of his wife's mother—Visit with E. Newport 1850—Building a house for the widow and fatherless—Visit with E. Newport 1852—Visit with E. Newport 1853 and 1854—Death of his sister Ruth—Marriage of his son—Visit with E. Newport in 1857—Drouth in the summer of 1858—Visit with E. Newport in 1861—Visit to Loudoun county, Virginia, 1867.

1845. First month 5th. Left home in my own conveyance as companion to Ann Weaver and Susanna Lower, on a religious visit to some of the meetings of Friends in Pennsylvania. We attended those of Wrightstown, Makefield, Buckingham Monthly Meeting held at Plumstead, Doylestown, and Solebury, and crossing the Delaware river, drove thirteen miles to Kingwood, N. J., and on the 9th attended that monthly meeting. In the afternoon we went fifteen miles on the way to Stroudsburg, and crossed the river on a boat the next morning at Otter's Ferry, and drove six miles up the river and through the Water Gap. A beautiful, romantic sight;—well worth a journey of fifty miles to any one fond of natural scenery! A further drive of four miles took us to Stroudsburg. The next three days we visited the families of Friends in that locality, attended their meeting on First-day morning, and had a meeting in the evening in the Court House. On the 13th we started for Richland, dining at Nazareth, nineteen miles, and twenty-two miles farther took us to our destination. At Richland we visited some of the families, and held a meeting in the evening. 14th. Rode eighteen miles to Gwynedd, had a meeting in the afternoon, and went to William Foulke's to supper, where I separated from my companions. William took Ann and Susanna to their homes, and I returned to mine and found the family well, but a favorite horse dead.

This year Texas was wrested from the Mexican Government and made one of the States of the Union, with a constitution that slavery shall never be abolished,—as though we could ignore the justice of the Almighty.

In the spring of 1846 my nearest neighbor, after three months' sickness and suffering (through which I nursed him faithfully), died, leaving a wife, four small children, and very limited means. As it was necessary these should be cared for, we took the youngest son, a nice little boy under seven years of age, and he remained with us until he was about eighteen; then he went to Philadelphia, became an apprentice in a large manufacturing establishment, and in a few years was one of the firm,—a striking instance of what honesty, industry, and integrity will accomplish. Another son and a daughter by a former marriage were provided for by the will of their maternal grandfather, and as the property had been in the family for generations, this son was desirous of retaining the possession of it, but as he was a minor I, being his guardian, bought it for him, and held it until he was of age, then deeded it to him; all very satisfactory. The farm was rented, and as the house could accommodate two families, the widow and children had a home there free of rent, and we favored them in every way we could. I have dwelt thus long on this because, for several years, next to my own family, they claimed much of my attention.

In the Tenth month of this year I accompanied Elizabeth Newport and Elizabeth Paxson on a religious visit to the families of Wrightstown Monthly Meeting. At this time Wrightstown Meeting was composed of one hundred and fifty-seven families and parts of families. (See "Memoirs of E. Newport," page 150.)

The following winter, one of our members being about to marry, applied to me to sell him a piece of land upon which to build a house. On conferring, we concluded to buy out a person already established in the same business. Finding he had no means except what was necessary to the continuance of his trade, which was that of a shoemaker, and that there was a mortgage of $800 on the property, I furnished the remaining $700 and took his note at 5 per cent. interest, without any security. He was a goodly, honest man and gradually the debt was cancelled. The last day of this year Mother Conard departed this life, and the following fall the farm was sold.

The years 1848-'49 were passed as many others have been in attending to home duties and sometimes in aiding our ministers in their religious services by taking them from one meeting to another in our carriages. In the Seventh month, 1850, I accompanied Elizabeth Newport and her companion to visit Friends in their families or meetings within the limits of Western Quarterly Meeting, Pa. (See "Memoirs," page 157.)

The time had now arrived in which I had realized the fulfillment of the covenant I made on my first setting out in life: that if I was favored to own a farm worth ten thousand dollars I would be satisfied, and not desire more. The day I made the last payment on the farm was one of thanksgiving and praise to my Heavenly Father for his many blessings vouchsafed to me. But now came the struggle. I was in a good way of making money and circumstances favored my continuing in the same way as heretofore. After some reflection I concluded to build a house for the widow and fatherless, which was done in the summer of 1851, at an expense of one thousand dollars over and above our own labor and the board of the workmen. The house, which was of stone, contained six rooms and a kitchen. The homestead of which I have before spoken having been sold out of the family, the widow and two children moved into the new home in the spring of 1852.

The following winter I accompanied Elizabeth Newport and Tacy Paxson on a religious visit to some of the meetings within the limits of Baltimore Yearly Meeting, and to many slave-holders and their families in various neighborhoods, which was kindly accepted by them. In these visits gospel truths were freely declared. We traveled in our own conveyance, and as the roads were often very bad, it was sometimes hard to endure. We went as far south as Winchester, Va., and were absent about six weeks. (For a fuller account see "Memoirs of Elizabeth Newport," page 184.)

After leaving Winchester, where we had meetings among Friends and others, we turned our faces towards the mountains, where for weeks and weeks we were entirely among strangers. This, together with having a mountainous country and strange roads to travel over, made us feel sad indeed, but we felt that we were in the line of our duty, and we never missed our way, or met with any serious accident. During all that long, tedious journey there was never a day or an hour in which I could not appeal to my Heavenly Father and say: "Thou knowest, O Father, I am endeavoring to serve thee." And now, though years have passed since that journey took place, I do not feel that the sin of omission or commission can be laid to my charge in the performance of it.

The unrighteousness of slavery still pressing upon the mind of Elizabeth Newport, she felt required to pay the slave-holders another visit, and she obtained from her respective meetings a minute for religious service in five or six of the Southern States. As she and I had always traveled together in near unity and sympathy, we became closely banded in the service. I had now many seasons of deep baptism and much searching of heart to know the mind of truth in regard to my accompanying her in this great and weighty undertaking,—for I did earnestly seek to be guided aright, and what added to the weight on my mind my wife did not approve of my going. She had let in the belief that if I did go I would not return alive. This was a sore trial to me, but I was deeply convinced that if I attended to the pointings of truth all would be right, both temporally and spiritually. Many of my friends encouraged me, especially my wife's sisters, whose kindness I can never forget.

We left our homes on the 5th of Twelfth month, 1853, and drove to Wilmington the first night. (See "Memoirs," page 217.)

On the 2d of Second month, 1854, according to previous arrangement, we were met at Maysville, Kentucky, by William W. and Lydia Longstreth, who took our places as companions for E. N., on her mission to New Orleans, we feeling permitted to return to our dear homes. We parted in much tenderness of feeling. About sunset Elizabeth Clinger and I took passage on board an Alleghany packet, expecting to reach Pittsburg in forty hours, but owing to the low state of the water we often

---

[1] In a letter received from his wife while engaged in this service, she writes: "Believing as I do, that nothing less than an impression of a duty required of thee to aid in this great work has called thee from home at this time, I am often with thee in spirit and feel truly desirous thee may be enabled to perform the part of the labor assigned to thee to the honor of the great Head of the Church, and be permitted to retutn to thy family with the sweet reward of 'peace."

ran aground and were more than ninety hours on the river, making a tedious passage, and as the horses would neither eat nor drink much, on account of the noise, it made it wearing on the mind. Finding we could not get to Pittsburg on that boat, all the passengers except ourselves got on another, and we would gladly have done so, but they would not take the horses and carriage, but told us another boat would be along in a few hours; and this proved to be the case, for about that time another made its appearance, on which we were taken and landed in Pittsburg on the 7th. Here I had thought of putting the horses and carriage on the cars and coming immediately to Philadelphia; but for this they asked forty dollars, so I concluded to try it in my own conveyance. Though the horses were in poor traveling order, owing to their having been so long on the boat, making the prospect of a journey of 300 miles quite formidable, we left Pittsburg about two o'clock, and came fifteen miles that day. The next two days we drove forty miles each day, and the two following days forty one. On the 14th we lodged at Joseph S. Walton's, Fallowfield, Pa., and were truly glad to be once more under a Friend's roof, it having been just seven weeks since we enjoyed that favor. The next day we came on to my brother-in-law's, Charles Thomas's, at the Valley. The roads were bad again, but by taking good care of the horses, they had improved.

On the 16th I reached my dear home, weary and worn, but with a peaceful mind, a little before night, and found my family all well, and I was in good health, for which favor I felt truly thankful. When I consider the many exposures and hardships we had to undergo, I fully believe the Almighty Power, whose very self is Love, bore us up and carried us through that arduous journey. No one can know or enter into feeling with such a concern as that was, unless they have passed through something similar; for it may truly be said that "seeing is believing, but feeling hath no fellow."

The year 1856 was an eventful one to us. Six of our friends, including our dear sister Ruth Thomas, were removed by death. On the 22d of the Fifth month, our son was married to Elizabeth, daughter of Watson and Margaret H. Twining, and the following summer he brought his wife to live under the same roof with us, the house having been enlarged to accommodate two families. William was to be the farmer, and we were to retire from business, and my sincere desire was that we might so walk by that Divine rule which is sufficient to govern us in all things, that neither they nor we might ever have cause to regret the arrangement.

On the 18th of First month, 1857, E. Newport, Margaret Hazelton, and I left home to attend Bucks Quarterly Meeting, and to visit the families of Makefield Monthly Meeting. Part of the time the weather was severely cold, in some places the thermometer standing 22° below zero. (See "Memoirs of Elizabeth Newport," page 288.)

The following summer was marked by a drouth of unusual length. For three months we had scarcely any rain; less than I ever knew for so long a period of time; but on the 4th of Eighth month we were favored with a fine shower, which was considered a great blessing. The ground had become so dry the grass was as dead as it is in winter. Corn and potatoes ceased to grow; the hay was cut and gathered, but did not make more than half a crop. But the rain came in time to save the corn and potatoes, so that there was a reasonable crop, especially of the latter, and the anxious ones, who had feared a season of want, were relieved. Thanks to an all-wise Providence!

I have thought it best to leave a little account of this drouth, that if the like should again occur the people may know that nothing new had happened.

On the 17th of Sixth month, 1861, I left home in company with E. Newport and Mary Evans, to attend Fishing Creek Half Year's Meeting and the meetings composing it. (For a fuller account see "Memoirs," page 248.)

In 1867 I again visited Loudoun county, Va., as companion for Joseph Horner, and in passing through the country and beholding the destruction caused by the late war, I was deeply impressed with the dreadful effects of slavery. No language can describe the heavy woes it has entailed upon the people, both white and colored.

CHAPTER V.

Religious visit to Ohio Yearly Meeting—Death of his wife—Family visits with M. E. Travilla to the members of Abington Monthly Meeting—Visits to the families of Westbury Monthly Meeting, L. I., as companion for M. E. T. and Martha Dodgson—His regular attendance at his own meeting—His interest in organizations of practical value in his neighborhood--His marriage to Harriet E. Stockly, of Philadelphia—Visits to meetings under an appointment of the Yearly Meeting's Committee on Education—Attends Ohio Yearly Meeting—Attends some meetings in the Western States—Attends Baltimore Yearly Meeting—His sickness there—His interest in the Public Library of Hatboro—Attends Genesee Yearly Meeting—Attends New York Yearly Meeting—Attends Baltimore Yearly Meeting.

OWING probably to his failing health, the manuscript here closes, but on several occasions afterward he accompanied different Friends who traveled in the cause of Truth, taking them in his own conveyance from place to place, and fully entering into the spiritual work in which they were enlisted; and many are the testimonies to his qualifications for the important service of elder in the church, which station he acceptably filled until his death.

CHARLES KIRK. 45

Our friend, Martha Dodgson, writes: "The first time I met Charles to be personally acquainted with him, was at Ohio Yearly Meeting, held at Salem, in 1871. He was companion for Perry John, and I for Sarah Hunt, and there was then a bond of near unity of feeling formed between us."

In the Tenth month, he and his wife attended the fiftieth anniversary of the marriage of George and Catharine M. Truman, of Philadelphia. At that time there was no railroad communication between Warminster and the city, and as Elizabeth's health was frail, her family thought she was not strong enough to bear the drive, but she was anxious to go and her husband arranged to take her. They reached there safely and she enjoyed the occasion. The next morning Charles returned home, she remaining to visit her brother and his family. The morning next ensuing, on going to her bedside, life was found to be extinct; so quietly had she passed away, that her brother and his wife, who occupied the adjoining room with the communicating door open, were not aware of it. She was a woman of much religious experience, useful in her neighborhood, helpful in times of sickness, a valuable elder of Horsham Monthly Meeting, and her sudden death was much lamented. She was brought to her home, and a few days after, amid a large company of relatives and friends, her body was consigned to its final resting place in Friends' burying ground at Warminster.

Martha Dodgson again writes: "In the summer of 1872, Martha E. Travilla made a religious visit to the families of Abington Monthly Meeting, Pa. Charles and I entered into the labor with her, and I can say that in that work we were truly a united band. In the fall of 1872 we were again companions with Martha in visiting the families of Wilmington Monthly Meeting, Del.,—an arduous concern."

In the fall of 1873 Charles accompanied the above Friends on a visit to the families of Westbury Monthly Meeting, L. I.

When not religiously engaged elsewhere, Charles Kirk was regularly found at the appointed hour in attendance at his own meeting, in which his gravity of deportment and solidity of countenance gave evidence that his mind was exercised on subjects relating to his highest welfare. In the latter part of his life he not unfrequently expressed his concern for the spiritual growth in the truth of his fellow members, and for the maintenance of the righteous testimonies as professed by Friends.

But while ardently attached to the Society of which he was a birthright and also a convinced member, and long one of its regularly appointed overseers, he sympathized with the faithful adherents in all denominations, and was often pleasantly associated with them in works affecting the best interests of the community. As a director of the public schools he labored long and faithfully, and in all other organizations of practical value in the locality in which he lived he took an active part until near the close of his life.

In the Third month, 1874, Charles Kirk was united in marriage to Harriet E. Stockly of Philadelphia. The ceremony took place at the house of Dillwyn and Susan M. Parrish, and was under the care of the Monthly Meeting of Friends of Philadelphia, held at Race street. Besides the Friends above mentioned, several dedicated servants of the Most High were present, among them Jane Johnson, Deborah F. Wharton, William and Sarah J. Sharpless, Ann A. Townsend, Lydia Gillingham, and others.

In the Seventh month next ensuing, Charles Kirk, accompanied by his wife, Jane D. Satterthwait, and Wm. Wade Griscom, visited the meetings of Concord Quarter, under an appointment of the Yearly Meeting's Committee on Education, to inquire into the condition of school property.

In the Eighth month of the same year, with the approval of Horsham Monthly Meeting, he accompanied his wife on a religious visit to Ohio Yearly Meeting. They received much kindness from those visited, and returned to their home under an humbling sense of the goodness of their Heavenly Father. Sixth month, 1875, they attended Burlington Quarterly Meeting held at Crosswicks, N. J., and in the Seventh month were furnished by their monthly meeting with minutes for religious labor in some of the Western States. The prospect of leaving home for so long a time as would be required for this service, brought a solemn covering over their minds, but day by day way was made for them in the hearts of the people, and after an absence of more than five weeks they were favored to return to their home, having with satisfaction attended the first Yearly Meeting held in Illinois, Indiana Yearly Meeting, most of the meetings in Iowa, several in Illinois and Indiana, and some in Ohio.

1876. The Yearly Meeting's Committee on Education appointed six of their number " to visit, as way opened, or as they felt their minds drawn, any and every section of the Yearly Meeting to aid in establishing schools or assist those already established, that' need help to enable them to continue; also to endeavor to stir up in the minds of its members a more active concern for the education of their children under the care of Friends, either in meeting, neighborhood, or family schools." Charles Kirk and wife being included in the appointment, in the Seventh month of this year, with others of the sub-committee, held a conference on the subject at Newtown Square, and in pursuance of the same concern, attended Western and Caln Quarters. In the former, no way was made for them to work at that time, but in the latter a general feeling of interest was manifested, and a committee appointed. Subsequently, conferences were held with the Friends of Woodbury, Upper Greenwich, and Mullica Hill, N. J., and Haddonfield Quarter was attended. There they met a full expression of unity, manifested by the appointment of a committee.

The same fall, 1876, with the sanction of their monthly meeting, they attended Baltimore Yearly Meeting. Before leaving home Charles contracted a heavy cold, and the weather being inclement, it increased until he was prostrated on a sick bed, and suffered greatly with oppression and weakness. It was a trial of his faith, but he was favored to bear it with patience and cheerfulness. He reached his home with difficulty, but with a feeling of peace and abounding gratitude to his Heavenly Father.

The early part of the succeeding winter the weather was very cold, and for six weeks the ground was covered with snow; but the temperature moderated, and bright sunshiny days shed lustre over the landscape, and Charles Kirk's home was enlivened by the presence of many dear friends, in whose cheerful society his social feelings were strengthened, and he realized the truth of the expression: "Iron sharpeneth iron; so a man sharpeneth the countenance of his friends." While he greatly appreciated having his friends visit him in his home, yet when alone with his family he was never gloomy or despondent, but unselfish and considerate of the comfort of those around him; when not actively engaged it was his custom to spend his time mostly in reading, or in listening, if another were the reader, to that only which was calculated to inform the mind and enrich the heart. His memory was remarkable. A thought once received into his mind was there to stay, and could be reproduced when wanted. He never seemed to forget anything. Long rows of figures once established in his memory were ever after quoted with accuracy. Scripture history was as familiar to him as the incidents of his daily life.

For many years he was a director of the Union Public Library of Hatboro, three miles from his home. To this institution he gave considerable attention and interest; he was for a long time on the purchasing committee, and was concerned to select only such books as were instructive and profitable.

In the Eighth month, 1878, he and his wife attended Philadelphia Quarterly Meeting, held at the Valley, Pa., and in Tenth month they united with other members of the Educational Committee in holding a conference at Kennett Square, which was an encouraging opportunity. While from home at this time he attended the First-day morning meeting at West Grove, Gwynedd Monthly Meeting, held at Plymouth, and the meetings at Quakertown and Stroudsburg, Pa. He had long desired to visit Friends in those sections of his own Quarter, and he felt richly repaid for the effort.

In the early part of Tenth month he and his wife spent eleven days very pleasantly among their friends and relatives in Maryland and Delaware. They attended the monthly meetings of Fallston and Baltimore, and the First-day meeting at Sandy Spring. While in Baltimore they were kindly entertained by Joseph J. and Anna T. Janney, where in the evening a number of Friends collected. While in Smyrna, Del., they made a call of unusual interest on their esteemed friend, Ann Denny, then nearly one hundred and one years of age. Her step was quick, her mind bright, and she retained her usual characteristics until her death, which occurred about two years after.

In the Sixth month, 1879, with minutes of unity from their monthly meeting, they attended Genesee Yearly Meeting, some of the meetings composing it, and Fishing Creek Half-Year's Meeting. The entire service was an interesting one, and they returned with the covering of peace, satisfied in having done what they felt was required of them.

On his birthdays, which occurred on the 10th of the Twelfth month, and also on the first day of each year, his children, grandchildren, and mostly one or two others of the family were usually collected in his home, and these re-unions he greatly enjoyed until his health became too frail to bear the excitement of anticipating them.

1880. The early part of this year they were several times at neighboring meetings under a feeling of apprehended duty. Accompanied by Dillwyn and Susan M. Parrish, they attended the three monthly meetings in Philadelphia, and mingled socially with many dear friends there and elsewhere, by which he felt his spiritual strength renewed, and a fresh impetus given to strive to live under the divine anointing. In the Second month, with the sanction of their friends, they attended Shrewsbury and Rahway Quarterly Meeting, N. J., and had a refreshing time, religiously and socially, and soon after, with others of the committee, they held satisfactory conferences on the subject of education at Byberry, Pa., Salem and Moorestown, N. J. Having obtained a minute for the purpose in the Fifth month, he accompanied his wife to New York Yearly Meeting, on which occasion they found kind entertainment at the house of their young friends, Robert and Tacie Willetts.

On the 20th of the same month, under an appointment of their quarterly meeting, they attended the First-day meeting at Norristown, also a circular meeting at the Valley, and remained a day or two with relatives there, very pleasantly.

In the following Tenth month minutes were granted them to attend Baltimore Yearly Meeting, which they experienced to be a season of divine favor, and they returned with a feeling of thankfulness to the Heavenly Father for the loving manifestations of friendship and affection bestowed upon them.

CHAPTER VI.

His strong testimony against the use of intoxicants—Attends Centre Quarterly Meeting—Death of a sister-in-law—Attends meetings under an appointment of the Yearly Meeting's Committee on Deficiencies—Death of Susan M. Parrish—Religious visit to Friends of Purchase Quarterly Meeting, N. Y.—Visits by appointment of his Yearly Meeting to many of its meetings—Attends Baltimore Yearly Meeting—Attends New York Yearly Meeting—Death of Dillwyn Parrish—His sudden illness—Attends his Yearly Meeting for the last time—Attends Salem Quarterly Meeting, N. J.—His last sickness—His release from earth.

HAVING from comparatively early life felt a strong restriction from the use of intoxicants of every kind, not being willing to use them even as a medicine, and feeling a deep concern for the welfare of others in this respect, when he was fearful there was danger of their falling victims to the use of ardent spirits, he was constrained to speak a word of caution or entreaty against this insidious indulgence, and to labor to reclaim them from it. When, therefore, he was placed upon the Yearly Meeting's Committee on Intoxicating Beverages, he accepted it as an opportunity to work more effectively in the cause of temperance, and he was often drawn out in fervent desires to his Heavenly Father for ability to labor more availingly for the advancement of this righteous testimony.

Therefore, in addition to his accustomed religious and secular duties, he now felt it incumbent upon him to assist in holding temperance conferences, and he not unfrequently expressed the wish that he had the tongue of a ready speaker, that he might impress upon every one the fearful consequences of an indulgence in this pernicious custom.

In the Ninth month, 1882, with minutes from their monthly meeting, he and his wife attended Centre Quarterly Meeting, Pa. On their return they found his sister-in-law, Rebecca J. Conard, who came during their absence, very sick at their house. She lived eight days after their return and closed a useful, unselfish life, in the 66th year of her age.

In the Eleventh month they attended Baltimore Quarterly Meeting held at Fallston, and spent a few days with relatives in the neighborhood.

In 1884, the Yearly Meeting's Committee " to consider the deficiencies as shown in the reports from the quarterly meetings," appointed a number of Friends, among them Charles Kirk and wife, to attend and appoint meetings throughout our Yearly Meeting, and a number were held in different localities, sometimes followed by conferences. At the close of this yearly meeting, their valued and beloved friend, Susan M. Parrish, at whose house they were lodging, and where they always found a home when occasion required, passed away from earth.

In the Tenth month of 1884, in company with others of the committee, they visited the meetings of West Chester, Birmingham, Goshen, Willistown, Newtown Square, and Providence and held conferences in accordance with their appointment, and in the latter part of the month, with minutes of unity from their monthly meeting, they made a satisfactory religious visit to Friends of Purchase Quarterly Meeting, held at Chappaqua, N. Y. While in the prosecution of this visit they were kindly cared for in the home of Moses and Esther Peirce and daughters, and in mingling with them and others of that locality they were renewed in friendly feeling and spiritual life.

1885. Those appointed by the Committee on Deficiencies were released, and a committee was named by the Yearly Meeting "to visit some of its branches to encourage Friends in a more faithful attention to the requirements of our Discipline, and upholding and sustaining the testimonies of our Religious Society." Charles Kirk being one of the committee, with his wife and other members visited all the monthly meetings in Bucks Quarter as they came in course, holding in addition appointed meetings at Carversville, Lambertville, Makefield, Yardleyville, and Edgewood. They were kindly received and hospitably entertained by friends in the different neighborhoods, and trusted their visits and labors were mutually helpful. When in the prosecution of the concern, the committee visited Warminster, a large company, mostly young married persons, assembled at his house, and it was felt to be an unusual occasion. Beginning with a social feeling, the interest gradually deepened until all were gathered under a solemn covering of divine love. The next morning a large and interesting meeting was held at the meeting-house, in which the spoken word was lively and edifying. Under the same appointment they united with others in visiting the meetings and holding conferences with Friends in the Western Quarter.

In the fall of this year, with minutes from Horsham Monthly Meeting they again attended Baltimore Yearly Meeting, and returned with a feeling of peace.

Charles Kirk was truly a social man, and mostly had a word of greeting for a passing neighbor. When at home he was frequently favored with the company of dear friends and relatives whose society he greatly valued and enjoyed.

1886. Second month. With others of the Yearly Meeting's Committee to visit their members, they attended Moorestown Meeting, held a conference with Friends in the afternoon, and in the evening met a religious gathering at the house of Wm. Dunn and Lydia L. Rogers. On their return they visited Mary S. Lippincott, then living in Camden, N. J., with whom Charles had a comfortable interview, they having been schoolmates in childhood, and life-long friends.

In the Fourth month, they obtained minutes for the service and attended New York Quarterly Meeting held at Brooklyn, on which occasion they were kindly entertained by Henry and Sarah M. Haviland, at whose house in the evening a precious little company assembled. In the afternoon they attended the meeting at Rutherford Place, N. Y., and in the evening met a large and interesting company of promising young people at the house of Wm. M. and Anna Jackson.

In the Fifth month he attended his Yearly Meeting with the exception of the first two sessions, an unusual thing for him. He was prevented by the death of his only surviving brother. Having served on the educational committee since its first appointment, thirteen years, and realizing that many faithful and able workers were enlisted in the cause, he felt that the time of his release had come and expressing this feeling in the Yearly Meeting he was excused from further committee service in the work. He was also released at that time from the Yearly Meeting's Visiting Committee.

On the 17th of Ninth month of this year his beloved friend, Dillwyn Parrish, was removed by death, in the 78th year of his age—an event which he felt most acutely.

On the 4th of First month, 1887, Charles Kirk was unexpectedly taken with congestion of the brain and liver. Five weeks of extreme weakness, attended by occasional pain in the head, followed, when he was again more seriously attacked and for ten days he was watched with close attention, not knowing what the result would be. His sweetness of spirit, quietness of mind, regular habits, and general soundness of constitution no doubt greatly aided in his recovery to comparative health. The experiences of his sick chamber can never be effaced from the memory of those who were privileged to share them. Peace presided over his home and his Heavenly Father was felt to be so near no anxiety was entertained about the future. Each day he numbered his blessings, and rejoiced in the goodness and mercy of Him " whose loving kindness is over all his works."

A portion of his physical strength returned, and in the Fifth month he was in his place at Yearly Meeting, as usual. Between the sessions he rested near-by to enable him to meet the fatigue, and when the duties of the day were over he found a comfortable home with the children of his friends, Jesse and Martha James.

Though continuing to be feeble in body, in 1888 he was again favored to attend his Yearly Meeting, which he esteemed a great privilege. During the remainder of the year he was mostly at home, contented and cheerful. As they came in course he attended his quarterly, monthly, and particular meetings, in which he always seemed alive to the importance of the occasion, and not unfrequently had a word of exhortation to the people.

In the Twelfth month he and his wife attended Salem Quarterly Meeting, held at Woodbury, N. J. This he felt to be a precious visit. The mingling with concerned Friends was helpful and encouraging to him. In the family of Wm. Wade and Sarah M. Griscom he found a sympathizing home, and he ever after retained a grateful recollection of the time spent with them and their children.

The 10th of the same month being the 89th anniversary of his birth, his children, grandchildren, and great-grandchildren were collected for the last time in his home; and all seemed to enjoy it.

Previous to this, on the 14th of Seventh month, 1889, his wife records: My dear husband has now been an invalid for more than two years and six months. For nearly a month he has been confined to the house, and for the last two weeks to his bed or couch, rarely sitting up, except to take his meals. I have been his constant companion and nurse, and mostly we are alone, and I cannot close my eyes to the fact that he is declining in physical vigor. Many kind friends manifest their helpful sympathy, and the Father's presence is felt to be near, keeping us from murmuring and enabling us to live under a sense of his past and present mercies. Peace is the covering of our spirits, often crowning our days with "seasons of refreshing from the presence of the Lord."

Eleventh month 11th. Since the 23d ult. Charles has mostly been confined to his bed, suffering greatly, but his mind is so bright, his memory so unfailingly correct, and his spiritual perceptions so clear, I cannot cherish discouragement. Our friends draw near us in our season of trial, and their loving sympathy, timely visits, and letters, are a great satisfaction and comfort. His patience and cheerfulness are constant, and the feeling pervading his sick room is a peaceful resignation to the divine will.

To his wife it was his custom in sickness and in health daily to speak of the uncertainty of time and of those things pertaining to the spiritual life. With her he shared the trial of his suffering sickness, and the sorrow of their coming separation, but through all he was favored to say: "Not my will, O Father, but thine, be done."

The last four weeks of his life his sufferings greatly increased, and all remedies administered gave only very temporary relief. He believed he "was waiting till his patience was perfected," and often said this was now the work given him to do. On one occasion he said to his nurse, "I am almost through. Life has nearly run out."

A day or two before his close, he seemed to have been admitted to a foretaste of the heavenly kingdom, saying, "I feel so happy." "I have been in a beautiful place." "All is love and kindness there." Being asked, "Was it heaven?" "I expect so," he replied, adding, "I cannot talk to thee, but I want thee to talk to me." A feeling of thanksgiving and praise filled my heart, to which I gave audible expression, afterward repeating a portion of the CIII. Psalm. He bowed his head several times in acknowledgment.

Having desired his last hours should not be disturbed by offering him soothing remedies, his wishes w, re respected. He was cognizant of all that occurred till the end came, and though he continued to suffer, yet not a murmur or impatient word escaped his lips.

About 12.30 o'clock p. m. on Third-day, the 11th of Third month, 1890, his spirit was released from earth, and on the following Seventh-day morning, his body, aged 89 years, 3 months, and 1 day, was interred in Friends' burying ground, Warminster, Pa., on which occasion a large and solemn meeting was held, in which beautiful and fitting testimonies were borne to his unselfish and exemplary life.

"Thou wilt keep him in perfect peace whose mind is stayed on thee: because he trusteth in thee." Isaiah, 26: 3.